Go For Dev

AUTOMATION AND EFFICIENCY

OLIVER LUCAS JR

TABLE OF CONTENTS

Chapter 1

Chapter 2

Chapter 3

Chapter 4

Chapter 5

Chapter 6

Chapter 7

Chapter 8

Chapter 9

Chapter 10

Preface

The world of DevOps is constantly evolving, and the tools and technologies that drive it are changing at an equally rapid pace. In this dynamic landscape, Go has emerged as a powerful language for building efficient, reliable, and scalable DevOps solutions. Its simplicity, concurrency features, and strong ecosystem make it an ideal choice for automating infrastructure, managing deployments, and improving collaboration.

This book, "Go for DevOps Automation and Efficiency," is designed to be your comprehensive guide to leveraging Go in your DevOps journey. Whether you're a seasoned DevOps engineer or just starting out, this book will provide you with the knowledge and practical skills you need to harness the power of Go for automation and efficiency gains.

Throughout these chapters, we'll explore the fundamentals of Go programming, delve into its application in key DevOps areas, and provide practical examples and best practices to guide you. You'll learn how to:

Automate system administration tasks: Manage processes, work with files and directories, and monitor system resources.

Build command-line tools: Create powerful and user-friendly CLIs for DevOps automation.

Manage networks: Automate network configuration, interact with cloud providers, and build network services.

Work with containers: Automate Docker builds and deployments, and manage container orchestration.

Implement configuration management: Extend configuration management tools and automate workflows.

Build CI/CD pipelines: Automate builds, tests, and deployments for continuous integration and delivery.

Monitor and observe systems: Integrate with monitoring systems, build custom monitoring tools, and implement effective logging.

By the end of this book, you'll be well-equipped to apply Go in your DevOps projects, automate your workflows, and improve the efficiency and reliability of your infrastructure and applications.

We believe that Go has the potential to revolutionize the way DevOps is practiced, and we're excited to share this knowledge with you. Let's dive in and explore the world of Go for DevOps!

Chapter 1

Introduction to Go for DevOps

1.1 Why Go is Ideal for DevOps

Go has rapidly become a favorite language in the DevOps world, and for good reason. Here's a breakdown of the key characteristics that make Go ideal for DevOps automation and efficiency:

1. Speed and Efficiency:

Compiled Language: Go compiles directly to machine code, resulting in very fast execution speeds. This is crucial for DevOps tools that need to perform tasks quickly and efficiently.

Lightweight: Go programs have a small memory footprint, making them ideal for running on servers and containers with limited resources.

2. Concurrency:

Goroutines: Go has built-in support for concurrency with goroutines, lightweight threads that allow you to perform multiple tasks simultaneously. This is essential for DevOps tasks like managing multiple servers, running parallel processes, and handling asynchronous operations.

Channels: Go provides channels for safe and efficient communication between goroutines, making it easier to write concurrent programs that are free from race conditions and deadlocks.

3. Simplicity and Readability:

Clean Syntax: Go has a clear and concise syntax that is easy to learn and read, even for developers new to the language. This reduces development time and makes it easier to maintain and debug code.

Small Standard Library: Go's standard library is comprehensive yet focused, providing all the essential tools for DevOps tasks without unnecessary complexity.

4. Cross-Platform Compatibility:

Build Once, Run Anywhere: Go programs can be compiled to run on various operating systems (Windows, Linux, macOS) and architectures. This makes it easy to deploy DevOps tools across different environments.

5. Excellent Tooling:

Built-in Testing Framework: Go has a built-in testing framework that simplifies unit testing and ensures code quality.

Strong Ecosystem: Go has a growing ecosystem of libraries and tools specifically designed for DevOps tasks, such as managing infrastructure, automating deployments, and monitoring systems.

6. DevOps-Specific Strengths:

Ideal for CLI tools: Go excels at building command-line interfaces (CLIs), which are essential for many DevOps tasks.

Great for networking: Go has strong support for network programming, making it suitable for tasks like building network services, automating network configuration, and interacting with APIs.

Microservices friendly: Go's lightweight nature and concurrency features make it well-suited for building and managing microservices architectures, a common pattern in modern DevOps.

By combining these advantages, Go empowers DevOps engineers to create robust, efficient, and maintainable automation solutions. It allows them to streamline workflows, improve system reliability, and increase overall productivity.

1.2 Setting Up Your Go Environment

Setting up your Go environment is the crucial first step to start developing with this powerful language. Here's a comprehensive guide to get you going:

1. Download and Install Go

Visit the official Go website: Head over to go.dev and download the appropriate installer for your operating system (Windows, macOS, Linux).

Run the installer: Follow the on-screen instructions to install Go. The default settings are usually fine.

Verify the installation: Open your terminal or command prompt and type `go version`. You should see the installed Go version printed, confirming a successful installation.

2. Set Up Your Workspace (GOPATH)

Understand GOPATH: `GOPATH` is an environment variable that tells Go where to find your source code, packages, and compiled binaries.

Choose a directory: Select a directory on your system to serve as your `GOPATH`. A common choice is `~/go` (or `%USERPROFILE%\go` on Windows).

Set the GOPATH environment variable:

On Linux/macOS: Add the following line to your shell's configuration file (e.g., `~/.bashrc` or `~/.zshrc`):

Bash

```
export GOPATH=$HOME/go
```

On Windows: Go to "Environment Variables" in your system settings and add a new system variable named GOPATH with the path to your chosen directory.

Create the necessary directories: Inside your GOPATH directory, create three subdirectories:

src: This is where your Go source code files will reside.

pkg: Go will store compiled package objects in this directory.

bin: This directory will hold compiled executable binaries.

3. Add Go Binaries to Your PATH

Why add to PATH?: Adding the GOPATH/bin directory to your PATH environment variable allows you to execute Go binaries from any location in your terminal.

Update your PATH:

On Linux/macOS: Add the following line to your shell's configuration file:

Bash

```
export PATH=$PATH:$GOPATH/bin
```

On Windows: Edit the `PATH` environment variable in your system settings and add the path to your `GOPATH/bin` directory.

4. Choose a Code Editor or IDE

Popular options:

Visual Studio Code (VS Code): A lightweight and highly extensible editor with excellent Go support through the official Go extension.

GoLand: A full-featured IDE by JetBrains specifically designed for Go development.

Sublime Text: A powerful text editor with good Go support through community packages.

Vim/Neovim: Highly configurable terminal-based editors with strong Go support through plugins.

Install a Go extension: If you're using an editor like VS Code, install the official Go extension to get features like code completion, debugging, and code navigation.

5. Test Your Setup

Create a simple Go program:

Go

```
package main

import "fmt"

func main() {
    fmt.Println("Hello, Go!")
}
```

Save the file: Save the code as `hello.go` inside a directory like `$GOPATH/src/hello`.

Run the program: Open your terminal, navigate to the directory containing `hello.go`, and run the command `go run hello.go`. You should see "Hello, Go!" printed in your terminal.

Congratulations! You have successfully set up your Go environment and are ready to start developing Go applications for DevOps automation.

1.3 Essential Go Syntax and Concepts for DevOps

1. Variables and Data Types

Declaring Variables: Go uses the `var` keyword to declare variables. You can specify the data type explicitly or let Go infer it.

Go

```
var message string = "Hello, DevOps!"
 var count int = 10
age := 30 // Type inference
```

Common Data Types:

`string`: For storing text.

`int`, `int32`, `int64`: For integer values.

`float32`, `float64`: For floating-point numbers.

`bool`: For boolean values (true or false).

2. Control Flow

Conditional Statements: Use `if`, `else if`, and `else` to control the flow of execution based on conditions.

Go

```
if age >= 18 {
    fmt.Println("You are an adult.")
} else {
    fmt.Println("You are a minor.")
}
```

Loops: Go provides `for` loops for iteration.

Go

```
for i := 0; i < 5; i++ {
    fmt.Println(i)
}
```

3. Functions

Defining Functions: Use the `func` keyword to define functions.

Go

```go
func greet(name string) {
    fmt.Println("Hello,", name)
}
```

Returning Values: Functions can return values using the `return` statement.

Go

```go
func add(x int, y int) int {
    return x + y
}
```

4. Packages

Importing Packages: Go uses the `import` keyword to include external packages.

Go

```go
import (
    "fmt"
    "os"
)
```

Standard Library: Go has a rich standard library with packages for various tasks (e.g., `fmt` for formatting, `os` for operating system interaction, `net/http` for networking).

5. Arrays and Slices

Arrays: Fixed-size collections of elements of the same data type.

Go

```
var numbers [5]int = [5]int{1, 2, 3, 4, 5}
```

Slices: Dynamically sized arrays that are more flexible.

Go

```
names := []string{"Alice", "Bob", "Charlie"}
```

6. Maps

Key-Value Pairs: Maps store data in key-value pairs.

Go

```
serverStatus := map[string]string{
    "server1": "running",
    "server2": "stopped",
}
```

7. Structs

Custom Data Structures: Structs allow you to define your own data types by grouping together different fields.

Go

```
type Server struct {
    Name    string
    IP      string
    Status  string
}
```

8. Pointers

Memory Addresses: Pointers hold the memory address of a value.

Indirect Access: Use pointers to modify the original value stored at a memory address.

9. Error Handling

Returning Errors: Go functions often return an error value to indicate success or failure.

Go

```
if err != nil {
    fmt.Println("Error:", err)
}
```

10. Concurrency (Goroutines and Channels)

Goroutines: Lightweight threads for concurrent execution.

Go

```
go func() {
    // Code to be executed concurrently
}()
```

Channels: Provide a way for goroutines to communicate and synchronize.

These essential Go syntax and concepts provide a solid foundation for writing effective DevOps automation scripts and tools. By mastering these fundamentals, you'll be well-equipped to tackle various DevOps challenges with Go.

Chapter 2

Automating System Administration with Go

2.1 Managing System Processes with Go

Go provides powerful tools for managing system processes, allowing you to automate tasks, control program execution, and interact with your operating system. Here's a breakdown of key concepts and techniques:

1. The `os/exec` **Package**

`exec.Command()`: This function creates a new `Cmd` struct representing an external command. You provide the command name and its arguments.

Go

```
cmd := exec.Command("ls", "-l")
```

`cmd.Run()`: Executes the command and waits for it to complete.

Go

```
err := cmd.Run()
if err != nil {
    fmt.Println("Error:", err)
```

```
}
```

`cmd.Output()`: Executes the command and captures its standard output.

Go

```go
out, err := cmd.Output()
if err != nil {
    fmt.Println("Error:", err)
}
fmt.Println(string(out))
```

`cmd.Start()` **and** `cmd.Wait()`: Starts the command in the background and then waits for it to finish. This gives you more control over the process.

Go

```go
err := cmd.Start()
// ... do other things while the command runs ...
err = cmd.Wait()
```

2. Handling Process Output

`Stdout` **and** `Stderr`: You can access the standard output and standard error streams of a command.

Go

```
cmd := exec.Command("mycommand")
cmd.Stdout = os.Stdout // Redirect output to the
terminal
cmd.Stderr = os.Stderr // Redirect errors to the
terminal
```

Pipes: Use pipes to connect the output of one command to the input of another.

Go

```
cmd1 := exec.Command("cat", "myfile.txt")
cmd2 := exec.Command("grep", "keyword")

pipe, _ := cmd1.StdoutPipe()
cmd2.Stdin = pipe
cmd2.Stdout = os.Stdout

cmd1.Start()
cmd2.Start()
cmd1.Wait()
cmd2.Wait()
```

3. Process Control

`cmd.Process.Pid`: Gets the process ID (PID) of the running command.

`cmd.Process.Kill()`: Terminates the process.

`cmd.Process.Signal()`: Sends a signal to the process (e.g., `syscall.SIGTERM` for graceful termination, `syscall.SIGKILL` for forced termination).

4. Working with System Signals

`os/signal` **package:** This package provides functions for handling system signals (e.g., `SIGINT` for Ctrl+C, `SIGTERM` for termination requests).

Go

```go
c := make(chan os.Signal)
signal.Notify(c, os.Interrupt, syscall.SIGTERM)

go func() {
    <-c // Wait for a signal
        fmt.Println("Received signal, cleaning
up...")
    // ... perform cleanup actions ...
    os.Exit(1)
}()
```

Example: Monitoring a Process

Go

```go
package main
```

```go
import (
    "fmt"
    "os/exec"
    "time"
)

func main() {
    cmd := exec.Command("ping", "google.com")
    err := cmd.Start()
    if err != nil {
        fmt.Println("Error starting command:", err)
        return
    }

    fmt.Printf("Process started with PID: %d\n", cmd.Process.Pid)

    go func() {
        time.Sleep(10 * time.Second)
        fmt.Println("Terminating process...")
        cmd.Process.Kill()
    }()

    err = cmd.Wait()
    if err != nil {
        fmt.Println("Process exited with error:", err)
    } else {
        fmt.Println("Process exited successfully")
    }
}
```

This example starts a `ping` command, gets its PID, and then terminates it after 10 seconds.

By mastering these techniques, you can effectively manage system processes in your Go DevOps scripts and tools, automating tasks and improving efficiency.

2.2 Working with Files and Directories

Go's standard library provides comprehensive tools for interacting with files and directories, making it well-suited for DevOps tasks that involve system administration, automation, and configuration management. Here's a breakdown of essential functions and techniques:

1. The `os` Package

`os.Open(filename)`: Opens a file for reading. Returns a `*File` object and an error if the file cannot be opened.

Go

```go
file, err := os.Open("myfile.txt")
if err != nil {
    // Handle error
}
defer file.Close() // Ensure the file is closed when done
```

`os.Create(filename)`: Creates a new file. If the file already exists, it will be truncated.

Go

```go
file, err := os.Create("newfile.txt")
if err != nil {
    // Handle error
}
defer file.Close()
```

os.Read(file): Reads data from a file into a byte slice.

Go

```go
data := make([]byte, 1024)
count, err := file.Read(data)
if err != nil {
    // Handle error
}
fmt.Println(string(data[:count]))
```

os.Write(file): Writes data to a file.

Go

```go
data := []byte("This is some text.")
_, err := file.Write(data)
if err != nil {
    // Handle error
}
```

`os.Close(file)`: Closes a file. It's important to close files to release resources.

2. The `ioutil` Package

`ioutil.ReadFile(filename)`: Reads the entire contents of a file into a byte slice. This is a convenient way to read small files.

Go

```go
data, err := ioutil.ReadFile("myfile.txt")
if err != nil {
    // Handle error
}
fmt.Println(string(data))
```

`ioutil.WriteFile(filename, data, perm)`: Writes data to a file. `perm` specifies the file permissions (e.g., `0644` for read/write for owner, read-only for others).

Go

```go
data := []byte("This is new content.")
err := ioutil.WriteFile("myfile.txt", data, 0644)
if err != nil {
    // Handle error
}
```

3. The `filepath` Package

`filepath.Join(path1, path2, ...)`: Joins multiple path components into a single path, correctly handling different operating system path separators.

Go

```
path    :=    filepath.Join("home",    "user",
"documents", "myfile.txt")
```

`filepath.Abs(path)`: Returns the absolute path of a file or directory.

`filepath.Base(path)`: Returns the base name (last element) of a path.

`filepath.Dir(path)`: Returns the directory portion of a path.

4. Directory Operations

`os.Mkdir(dirname, perm)`: Creates a new directory.

`os.MkdirAll(dirname, perm)`: Creates a directory and any necessary parent directories.

`os.Remove(filename)`: Deletes a file.

`os.RemoveAll(dirname)`: Deletes a directory and its contents.

`os.Rename(oldpath, newpath)`: Renames a file or directory.

`os.Stat(filename)`: Returns a `FileInfo` struct containing information about a file or directory (e.g., size, permissions, modification time).

Example: Copying a File

Go

```go
package main

import (
    "fmt"
    "io"
    "os"
)

func copyFile(src, dst string) error {
    sourceFile, err := os.Open(src)
    if err != nil {
        return err
    }
    defer sourceFile.Close()

    destFile, err := os.Create(dst)
    if err != nil {
        return err
    }
    defer destFile.Close()

    _, err = io.Copy(destFile, sourceFile)
    if err != nil {
        return err
    }

    return nil
```

```
}

func main() {
    err            :=            copyFile("source.txt",
"destination.txt")
    if err != nil {
        fmt.Println("Error copying file:", err)
    } else {
        fmt.Println("File                     copied
successfully!")
    }
}
```

This example demonstrates how to copy a file using `os.Open`, `os.Create`, and `io.Copy`.

By combining these file and directory operations, you can build powerful Go programs for DevOps automation. You can read configuration files, write logs, manage deployments, and perform many other tasks related to file system manipulation.

2.3 Automating System Monitoring and Alerting

Go's strengths in concurrency, networking, and system interaction make it a powerful tool for automating system monitoring and alerting tasks. Here's how you can leverage Go to build robust monitoring and alerting systems:

1. Collect System Metrics

Use the `os` **package:** Gather system information like CPU usage, memory usage, disk space, and network statistics using functions like `os.Hostname()`, `os.Getenv()`, and by reading files in `/proc` (on Linux).

Third-party libraries: Explore libraries like `gopsutil` (cross-platform system information) and `shirou/gopsutil` (process and system utilization) for more advanced metrics collection.

2. Monitor Resources and Services

Check process status: Use `exec.Command()` to execute commands like `ps` or `top` to monitor running processes and their resource consumption.

Ping services: Use `net.Dial()` or `exec.Command("ping", ...)` to check the availability of network services.

Monitor logs: Read and analyze log files for errors, warnings, or specific patterns that indicate issues.

3. Implement Alerting Mechanisms

Email notifications: Use the `net/smtp` package to send email alerts when critical conditions are detected.

Slack notifications: Integrate with Slack's API using a library like `slack-go/slack` to send alerts to Slack channels.

PagerDuty integration: Use PagerDuty's API to trigger incidents and notify on-call personnel.

Webhooks: Send HTTP POST requests to webhooks to trigger actions in other systems.

4. Design Alerting Rules

Thresholds: Define thresholds for metrics (e.g., CPU usage > 80%, disk space < 10%) to trigger alerts.

Anomaly detection: Use statistical analysis or machine learning techniques to identify unusual patterns in metrics and trigger alerts.

Custom logic: Implement custom Go functions to define complex alerting rules based on your specific needs.

5. Build a Monitoring Daemon

Run in the background: Use goroutines and channels to create a monitoring daemon that runs continuously in the background.

Periodic checks: Use `time.Ticker` or `time.Sleep()` to perform checks at regular intervals.

Error handling: Implement robust error handling to prevent the monitoring daemon from crashing.

Example: Simple CPU Usage Monitor

Go

```go
package main

import (
    "fmt"
    "time"

    "github.com/shirou/gopsutil/cpu"
)

func main() {
    for {
        percentages,                err            :=
cpu.Percent(time.Second, true)
        if err != nil {
            fmt.Println("Error    getting    CPU
usage:", err)
        }
```

```go
        for i, cpuPercent := range percentages
{
            fmt.Printf("CPU %d: %.2f%%\n", i,
cpuPercent)
            if cpuPercent > 80 {
                // Send alert (e.g., email,
Slack)
                fmt.Println("ALERT: High CPU
usage on CPU", i)
            }
        }

        time.Sleep(5 * time.Second)
    }
}
```

This example uses the `gopsutil` library to get CPU usage every 5 seconds. If any CPU core exceeds 80% usage, it prints an alert message (you would replace this with your actual alerting logic).

By combining these techniques and leveraging Go's strengths, you can create efficient and reliable systems for automating system monitoring and alerting, ensuring the health and stability of your infrastructure.

Chapter 3

Go and the Command Line

3.1 Building CLI Tools with Go

Go is a fantastic language for building command-line interface (CLI) tools due to its speed, simplicity, and strong standard library. Here's a guide to get you started:

1. The `flag` Package

Defining Flags: Use `flag.String()`, `flag.Int()`, `flag.Bool()`, etc., to define flags for your CLI tool.

Go

```
import "flag"

var namePtr = flag.String("name", "World", "A name to say hello to.")
var agePtr = flag.Int("age", 42, "An age.")
```

Parsing Flags: Call `flag.Parse()` to parse the command-line arguments and populate the flag variables.

Go

```
func main() {
    flag.Parse()
```

```go
    fmt.Println("Hello", *namePtr)
    fmt.Println("Age:", *agePtr)
}
```

Usage: Run your program with flags like this: `./myprogram -name="Go" -age=20`

2. Handling User Input

`os.Args`: This slice holds the command-line arguments. `os.Args[0]` is the program name, and subsequent elements are the arguments.

Go

```go
if len(os.Args) < 2 {
    fmt.Println("Usage: myprogram <argument>")
    os.Exit(1)
}
argument := os.Args[1]
```

`bufio.NewReader(os.Stdin)`: Use this to read input from the user interactively.

Go

```go
reader := bufio.NewReader(os.Stdin)
fmt.Print("Enter your name: ")
```

```
name, _ := reader.ReadString('\n')
```

3. Structuring Your CLI

Subcommands: For complex CLIs, use subcommands to organize functionality. You can use the `flag` package or third-party libraries like `spf13/cobra` or `urfave/cli` to create subcommands.

Go

```go
// Using spf13/cobra (example)
var rootCmd = &cobra.Command{
    Use:   "mycli",
        Short: "A brief description of your application",
}

var greetCmd = &cobra.Command{
    Use:   "greet",
    Short: "Greet someone",
     Run: func(cmd *cobra.Command, args []string)
{
        // ... greet logic ...
    },
}

func main() {
    rootCmd.AddCommand(greetCmd)
    if err := rootCmd.Execute(); err != nil {
        fmt.Println(err)
        os.Exit(1)
```

```
        }
}
```

4. Output and Formatting

`fmt.Println()`: For basic output.

`fmt.Printf()`: For formatted output using verbs (e.g., %s, %d).

`text/tabwriter`: For creating formatted tables.

Coloring: Use ANSI escape codes or libraries like `fatih/color` to add colors to your output.

5. Error Handling

Return errors: Use Go's error handling mechanism (`if err != nil { ... }`) to handle errors gracefully.

Exit codes: Use `os.Exit(1)` to signal an error to the shell.

Informative messages: Provide clear and helpful error messages to the user.

Example: Simple File Counter

Go

```go
package main

import (
    "flag"
    "fmt"
    "io/ioutil"
)

func main() {
```

```go
    filePath := flag.String("file", "", "Path to
the file")
    flag.Parse()

    if *filePath == "" {
        fmt.Println("Usage:          filecounter
-file=<filename>")
        return
    }

    data, err := ioutil.ReadFile(*filePath)
    if err != nil {
        fmt.Println("Error reading file:", err)
        return
    }

    fmt.Printf("File    size:    %d    bytes\n",
len(data))
}
```

This example defines a `-file` flag to take a file path as input and then prints the size of the file in bytes.

These techniques provide a foundation for building powerful and user-friendly CLI tools in Go. By combining these with Go's concurrency features and external libraries, you can create sophisticated CLIs for DevOps automation and other tasks.

3.2 Handling Command-Line Arguments and Flags

Handling command-line arguments and flags effectively is crucial for creating user-friendly and flexible Go CLI tools. Here's a breakdown of how to work with them:

1. The os Package for Basic Arguments

os.Args: This slice holds all the command-line arguments passed to your program.

os.Args[0] is always the program name itself.

os.Args[1] onwards are the user-provided arguments.

Go

```go
package main

import (
    "fmt"
    "os"
)

func main() {
    if len(os.Args) != 2 {
                fmt.Println("Usage:    myprogram
<filename>")
        os.Exit(1)
    }
    filename := os.Args[1]
    fmt.Println("Processing file:", filename)
}
```

2. The `flag` Package for Flags

Defining flags:

`flag.String("name", "default", "usage message")`: String flag.

`flag.Int("count", 10, "usage message")`: Integer flag.

`flag.Bool("verbose", false, "usage message")`: Boolean flag.

`flag.Var(value, "name", "usage message")`: For custom flag types.

Go

```
import "flag"

var name = flag.String("name", "Guest", "Name to greet")
var age = flag.Int("age", 30, "Age of the person")
```

Parsing flags:

`flag.Parse()`: Parses the command-line arguments and sets the flag values. Must be called before accessing flag values.

Go

```go
func main() {
    flag.Parse()
    fmt.Println("Hello,", *name)
    fmt.Println("Age:", *age)
}
```

Accessing flag values:

Access the values of flags using the pointers returned by the flag functions (e.g., *name, *age).

Usage:

Run your program with flags like this: ./myprogram -name="Alice" -age=25

3. Advanced Flag Handling

Short flags: Use a single dash followed by a single character (e.g., -n "Alice"). Define short flags in the flag definition: flag.String("name", "Guest", "Name to greet").

Combining flags: Combine single-character flags (e.g., ./myprogram -n "Alice" -a 25 is the same as ./myprogram -na "Alice" 25).

Custom flag types: Implement the flag.Value interface to create your own flag types.

4. Best Practices

Clear usage messages: Provide informative usage messages for your flags using the third argument in the flag definition functions.

Consistent flag names: Use lowercase letters and hyphens for flag names (e.g., `--output-file`).

Default values: Provide sensible default values for your flags.

Validation: Validate flag values after parsing to ensure they are within acceptable ranges or meet specific criteria.

Example with `os.Args` **and** `flag`

Go

```go
package main

import (
    "flag"
    "fmt"
    "os"
)

func main() {
    wordPtr := flag.String("word", "default", "The word to repeat")
    countPtr := flag.Int("count", 5, "Number of times to repeat the word")
    flag.Parse()

    if len(os.Args) < 2 {
        fmt.Println("Usage:          repeater [--word=<word>] [--count=<count>]")
        os.Exit(1)
    }

    for i := 0; i < *countPtr; i++ {
        fmt.Println(*wordPtr)
    }
}
```

This example combines `os.Args` to check for arguments and `flag` to handle optional flags.

By mastering these techniques, you can build robust and user-friendly CLI tools in Go that are easy to use and configure.

3.3 Interacting with Shell Commands and Scripts

Go provides excellent support for interacting with shell commands and scripts, allowing you to leverage existing tools and automate complex workflows within your Go programs. Here's how you can do it:

1. The `os/exec` Package

`exec.Command()`: This function creates a new `Cmd` struct representing an external command. You provide the command name and its arguments.

Go

```go
cmd := exec.Command("ls", "-l", "/home/user")
```

`cmd.Output()`: Executes the command and captures its standard output.

Go

```go
out, err := cmd.Output()
```

41

```go
if err != nil {
    fmt.Println("Error:", err)
}
fmt.Println(string(out)) // Print the output of
the command
```

`cmd.Run()`: Executes the command and waits for it to complete. Useful when you don't need to capture the output.

Go

```go
err := cmd.Run()
if err != nil {
    fmt.Println("Error:", err)
}
```

2. Running Shell Scripts

Execute scripts directly: You can execute shell scripts directly using `exec.Command()`.

Go

```go
cmd := exec.Command("./my_script.sh", "arg1",
"arg2")
err := cmd.Run()
// ... handle errors ...
```

Specify the interpreter: If your script doesn't have execute permissions or you need to use a specific interpreter (e.g., Bash, Python), you can specify it explicitly.

Go

```
cmd := exec.Command("bash", "-c", "./my_script.sh
arg1 arg2")
err := cmd.Run()
// ... handle errors ...
```

3. Passing Input to Commands

`cmd.Stdin`: Use this field to provide input to the command. You can use pipes or strings.

Go

```
cmd := exec.Command("grep", "keyword")
cmd.Stdin = strings.NewReader("This is a line of
text.\nAnother line with the keyword.\n")
out, _ := cmd.Output()
// ... process the output ...
```

4. Handling Output and Errors

`cmd.Stdout`, `cmd.Stderr`: Access the standard output and standard error streams of the command. You can redirect them to files, the console, or process them programmatically.

Go

```go
cmd := exec.Command("mycommand")
cmd.Stdout = os.Stdout // Redirect output to the
terminal
cmd.Stderr = os.Stderr // Redirect errors to the
terminal

var out bytes.Buffer
cmd.Stdout = &out // Capture output in a buffer
err := cmd.Run()
// ... process the output from the buffer ...
```

5. Environment Variables

`cmd.Env`: Set environment variables for the command.

Go

```go
cmd := exec.Command("mycommand")
cmd.Env = append(os.Environ(), "MY_VAR=value")
```

Example: Running a `date` command and capturing the output

Go

```go
package main

import (
    "fmt"
    "os/exec"
)

func main() {
    cmd := exec.Command("date", "+%Y-%m-%d")
    out, err := cmd.Output()
    if err != nil {
        fmt.Println("Error:", err)
        return
    }
    fmt.Println("Current date:", string(out))
}
```

This example runs the `date` command with a format specifier, captures the output, and prints it.

By using these techniques, you can seamlessly integrate shell commands and scripts into your Go programs, enabling powerful automation and interaction with the underlying operating system. This is particularly valuable for DevOps tasks like system administration, configuration management, and building deployment pipelines.

Chapter 4

Networking Automation with Go

4.1 Network Programming Fundamentals in Go

1. Core Concepts

Networks: A way to connect devices and allow them to communicate. This usually involves protocols (rules for communication) and addresses (unique identifiers for devices).

IP Addresses: Unique addresses that identify devices on a network (e.g., 192.168.1.100).

Ports: Numbered communication endpoints on a device. Different ports are used for different services (e.g., port 80 for web traffic, port 22 for SSH).

Protocols: Sets of rules for how devices communicate. Common protocols include:

TCP (Transmission Control Protocol): Reliable, connection-oriented communication. Used for things like web browsing, file transfer, and email.

UDP (User Datagram Protocol): Connectionless, less reliable but faster. Used for things like streaming video and gaming.

2. Key Go Packages

`net`: The core package for network programming in Go. It provides types and functions for working with network addresses, connections, and protocols.

`net/http`: For building web servers and clients.

`net/rpc`: For remote procedure calls (RPC).

3. Sockets

What are sockets? Sockets are the fundamental building blocks for network communication. They represent an endpoint for communication between two processes.

Creating sockets: You use functions like `net.Listen()` (for servers) and `net.Dial()` (for clients) to create sockets.

4. TCP Communication

Server:

Listen: Create a listener socket using `net.Listen("tcp", ":8080")`.

Accept: Accept incoming connections using `listener.Accept()`.

Read/Write: Read from and write to the connection using the `net.Conn` object.

Close: Close the connection when done.

Client:

Dial: Connect to the server using `net.Dial("tcp", "localhost:8080")`.

Read/Write: Read from and write to the connection using the `net.Conn` object.

Close: Close the connection when done.

5. UDP Communication

Server:

Listen: Create a listener using `net.ListenPacket("udp", ":5000")`.

ReadFrom: Read data from the socket using `listener.ReadFrom()`.

WriteTo: Send data to a specific address using `listener.WriteTo()`.

Close: Close the listener when done.

Client:

Dial: (Optional) Create a connected socket using `net.DialUDP("udp", nil, &net.UDPAddr{IP: net.ParseIP("localhost"), Port: 5000})`.

WriteTo: Send data to the server using `socket.WriteTo()`.

ReadFrom: Read data from the socket using `socket.ReadFrom()`.

Close: Close the socket when done.

6. Important Considerations

Error Handling: Network operations can fail, so always check for errors returned by functions.

Concurrency: Use goroutines to handle multiple connections concurrently, especially in server applications.

Security: Be mindful of security concerns when writing network applications. Consider using TLS/SSL for encryption.

Example: Simple TCP Server and Client

Go

```
// server.go
package main
```

```go
import (
    "fmt"
    "net"
)

func handleConnection(conn net.Conn) {
    defer conn.Close()
    buf := make([]byte, 1024)
    n, err := conn.Read(buf)
    if err != nil {
        fmt.Println("Error reading:", err)
        return
    }
    fmt.Println("Received:", string(buf[:n]))
    conn.Write([]byte("Message received."))
}

func main() {
    listener, err := net.Listen("tcp", ":8080")
    if err != nil {
        fmt.Println("Error listening:", err)
        return
    }
    defer listener.Close()

    for {
        conn, err := listener.Accept()
        if err != nil {
            fmt.Println("Error    accepting:", err)
            return
        }
        go handleConnection(conn)
    }
}
```

Go

```go
// client.go
package main

import (
    "fmt"
    "net"
)

func main() {
    conn, err := net.Dial("tcp",
"localhost:8080")
    if err != nil {
        fmt.Println("Error dialing:", err)
        return
    }
    defer conn.Close()

    conn.Write([]byte("Hello from client!"))
    buf := make([]byte, 1024)
    n, err := conn.Read(buf)
    if err != nil {
        fmt.Println("Error reading:", err)
        return
    }
    fmt.Println("Server response:",
string(buf[:n]))
}
```

This example demonstrates a basic TCP server that listens for connections and echoes back messages, and a client that sends a message and receives the response.

These fundamentals provide a solid starting point for network programming in Go. As you explore further, you can delve into more advanced topics like HTTP, websockets, RPC, and network security.

4.2 Building Network Services and Clients

Go excels at building network services and clients due to its built-in concurrency features (goroutines), efficient networking libraries, and focus on simplicity. Here's how you can create robust network applications in Go:

1. Choose the Right Protocol

TCP:

Reliable, ordered, and connection-oriented.

Ideal for applications that require guaranteed delivery and order of data, such as file transfer, web servers, and email.

UDP:

Connectionless and less reliable, but faster.

Suitable for applications where speed is more important than guaranteed delivery, such as streaming video, gaming, and DNS lookups.

2. Building TCP Servers

Listen for connections: Use `net.Listen("tcp", ":port")` to create a listener on a specific port.

Accept connections: Use `listener.Accept()` in a loop to accept incoming connections.

Handle connections concurrently: Use goroutines to handle each connection in a separate thread, preventing blocking and improving performance.

Read and write data: Use `conn.Read()` and `conn.Write()` to communicate with the client.

Close connections: Close the connection using `conn.Close()` when communication is complete.

Example TCP Server:

Go

```go
package main

import (
    "fmt"
    "net"
)

func handleConnection(conn net.Conn) {
    defer conn.Close()
    buf := make([]byte, 1024)
    n, err := conn.Read(buf)
    if err != nil {
        fmt.Println("Error reading:", err)
        return
    }
    fmt.Printf("Received    from    %s:    %s\n",
conn.RemoteAddr(), string(buf[:n]))
    conn.Write([]byte("Message received."))
}

func main() {
    listener, err := net.Listen("tcp", ":8080")
    if err != nil {
        fmt.Println("Error listening:", err)
```

```go
        return
    }
    defer listener.Close()

    for {
        conn, err := listener.Accept()
        if err != nil {
            fmt.Println("Error    accepting:",
err)
            return
        }
        go handleConnection(conn)
    }
}
```

3. Building TCP Clients

Connect to the server: Use `net.Dial("tcp", "address:port")` to establish a connection to the server.

Send data: Use `conn.Write()` to send data to the server.

Receive data: Use `conn.Read()` to receive data from the server.

Close the connection: Use `conn.Close()` to close the connection when done.

Example TCP Client:

Go

```go
package main

import (
    "fmt"
    "net"
)
```

```go
func main() {
    conn, err := net.Dial("tcp",
"localhost:8080")
    if err != nil {
        fmt.Println("Error dialing:", err)
        return
    }
    defer conn.Close()

    conn.Write([]byte("Hello from client!"))
    buf := make([]byte, 1024)
    n, err := conn.Read(buf)
    if err != nil {
        fmt.Println("Error reading:", err)
        return
    }
    fmt.Println("Server response:",
string(buf[:n]))
}
```

4. Building UDP Services

Listen for packets: Use `net.ListenPacket("udp", ":port")` to create a packet listener.

Read packets: Use `listener.ReadFrom()` to receive data from clients.

Send packets: Use `listener.WriteTo()` to send data to a specific client address.

Close the listener: Use `listener.Close()` to close the listener when done.

5. Building UDP Clients

Create a socket: Use `net.DialUDP("udp", localAddr, remoteAddr)` to create a UDP socket.

Send packets: Use `socket.WriteTo()` to send data to the server.

Receive packets: Use `socket.ReadFrom()` to receive data from the server.

Close the socket: Use `socket.Close()` to close the socket when done.

6. Important Considerations

Error handling: Always check for errors returned by network functions.

Timeouts: Implement timeouts to prevent your application from hanging indefinitely.

Buffers: Use appropriately sized buffers for reading and writing data to avoid performance issues.

Protocols: Define clear protocols for communication between your services and clients.

By following these guidelines and using Go's efficient networking libraries, you can build robust and scalable network services and clients for a wide range of applications.

4.3 Automating Network Configuration and Management

1. Key Go Packages and Tools

`net`: The foundation for network operations.

`golang.org/x/crypto/ssh`: For secure shell (SSH) connections to network devices.

`github.com/google/go-cmp/cmp`: For comparing configurations (useful for detecting changes).

APIs and SDKs: Many network device vendors (Cisco, Juniper, Arista, etc.) and cloud providers (AWS, Azure, GCP) offer Go APIs or SDKs for programmatic management.

2. Common Automation Tasks

Configuration backups:

Connect to devices via SSH.

Retrieve configuration files using commands like `show running-config`.

Store configurations in a version control system (Git) or a centralized database.

Configuration changes:

Generate configuration templates (using Go's `text/template` package).

Push configurations to devices using SSH and commands like `configure terminal`.

Verify changes by comparing the new configuration with the intended state.

Device provisioning:

Automate the initial configuration of new network devices.

Use Go to interact with APIs to provision devices in the cloud.

Network monitoring:

Collect network device metrics (CPU, memory, interface statistics).

Monitor network health and performance.

Trigger alerts based on predefined thresholds.

3. Example: Backing Up a Cisco Switch Configuration

Go

```go
package main

import (
    "fmt"
    "golang.org/x/crypto/ssh"
    "io/ioutil"
)

func main() {
    config := &ssh.ClientConfig{
        User: "username",
        Auth: []ssh.AuthMethod{
            ssh.Password("password"),
        },
        HostKeyCallback:
ssh.InsecureIgnoreHostKey(), // Use with caution
in production
    }

    client, err := ssh.Dial("tcp",
"switch-ip:22", config)
    if err != nil {
        panic(err)
    }
    defer client.Close()

    session, err := client.NewSession()
    if err != nil {
        panic(err)
    }
    defer session.Close()
```

```go
    out,   err   :=   session.CombinedOutput("show
running-config")
    if err != nil {
        panic(err)
    }

    err = ioutil.WriteFile("switch-config.txt",
out, 0644)
    if err != nil {
        panic(err)
    }

    fmt.Println("Configuration        saved        to
switch-config.txt")
}
```

This example connects to a Cisco switch via SSH, retrieves the running configuration using the `show running-config` command, and saves it to a file.

4. Important Considerations

Security: Use strong passwords or SSH keys for authentication.

Idempotency: Design your automation scripts to be idempotent (i.e., running them multiple times has the same effect as running them once). This prevents unintended changes.

Error handling: Implement robust error handling to gracefully handle network issues or device failures.

Testing: Thoroughly test your automation scripts in a staging environment before deploying them to production.

By combining Go's strengths with the right tools and techniques, you can effectively automate network configuration and management tasks. This can significantly improve efficiency, reduce errors, and free up network engineers to focus on more strategic initiatives.

Chapter 5

Go for Cloud Infrastructure Automation

5.1 Interacting with Cloud Providers (AWS, Azure, GCP)

Go is a powerful language for interacting with cloud providers like AWS, Azure, and GCP due to its excellent support for APIs, concurrency, and efficient network communication. Here's a breakdown of how to use Go with these platforms:

1. Authentication and Authorization

API Keys and Secrets: Most cloud providers use API keys and secrets for authentication. Securely store these credentials and use them to generate authentication tokens.

IAM Roles and Service Accounts: For more advanced scenarios, leverage IAM roles (AWS) or service accounts (GCP) to grant your Go applications specific permissions to cloud resources.

2. Using Cloud SDKs

AWS SDK for Go: `github.com/aws/aws-sdk-go` provides a comprehensive set of libraries for interacting with various AWS services (EC2, S3, Lambda, etc.).

```
Go

import (
```

```go
    "github.com/aws/aws-sdk-go/aws"

    "github.com/aws/aws-sdk-go/aws/session"

    "github.com/aws/aws-sdk-go/service/s3"
)


sess, _ := session.NewSession(&aws.Config{

    Region: aws.String("us-west-2"),

})


svc := s3.New(sess)

// ... use svc to interact with S3 ...
```

Azure SDK for Go: `github.com/Azure/azure-sdk-for-go`
offers a similar set of libraries for managing Azure resources.

Go

```go
import (

    "github.com/Azure/azure-sdk-for-go/sdk/azidentity"
```

```go
    "github.com/Azure/azure-sdk-for-go/sdk/resourcema
nager/compute/armcompute"

)



cred,                           _                          :=
azidentity.NewDefaultAzureCredential(nil)

client,                         _                          :=
armcompute.NewVirtualMachinesClient("subscription
ID", cred, nil)

// ... use client to manage virtual machines ...
```

Google Cloud Client Libraries for Go: cloud.google.com/go provides idiomatic Go libraries for accessing Google Cloud services (Compute Engine, Cloud Storage, BigQuery, etc.).

```go
Go

import (

    "cloud.google.com/go/storage"

    "context"

)



ctx := context.Background()
```

```go
client, _ := storage.NewClient(ctx)

// ... use client to interact with Cloud Storage
...
```

3. Common Use Cases

Infrastructure Management:

Provision and manage virtual machines, networks, and storage.

Automate deployments using Infrastructure-as-Code (IaC) tools like Terraform, which often have Go providers.

Data Storage and Processing:

Interact with cloud storage services (S3, Azure Blob Storage, Google Cloud Storage) to store and retrieve data.

Use serverless computing platforms (AWS Lambda, Azure Functions, Google Cloud Functions) to process data.

Monitoring and Logging:

Integrate with cloud monitoring and logging services (CloudWatch, Azure Monitor, Cloud Logging) to collect metrics and logs from your applications.

4. Example: Listing S3 Buckets

```go
Go

package main


import (
```

```go
    "fmt"

    "github.com/aws/aws-sdk-go/aws"

    "github.com/aws/aws-sdk-go/aws/session"

    "github.com/aws/aws-sdk-go/service/s3"
)


func main() {

    sess, err := session.NewSession(&aws.Config{

        Region:   aws.String("us-west-2"),   //
Replace with your region

    })

    if err != nil {

        fmt.Println("Error  creating  session:",
err)

        return

    }


    svc := s3.New(sess)


    result, err := svc.ListBuckets(nil)

    if err != nil {
```

```go
        fmt.Println("Error   listing   buckets:",
err)

        return

    }


    fmt.Println("Buckets:")

    for _, b := range result.Buckets {

        fmt.Printf("*   %s   created   on   %s\n",
aws.StringValue(b.Name),
aws.TimeValue(b.CreationDate))

    }

}
```

This example uses the AWS SDK for Go to list all S3 buckets in a specific region.

5. Important Considerations

Error Handling: Cloud APIs can return various errors. Implement robust error handling to gracefully handle failures.

Rate Limiting: Be aware of rate limits imposed by cloud providers and implement strategies to handle them (e.g., retries with exponential backoff).

Security: Follow security best practices for managing cloud credentials and accessing cloud resources.

By leveraging Go's strengths and the official cloud SDKs, you can efficiently interact with cloud providers, automate tasks, and build powerful cloud-native applications.

5.2 Managing Cloud Resources Programmatically

Managing cloud resources programmatically is essential for efficient and scalable cloud operations. Go, with its strong support for APIs and concurrency, is well-suited for this task. Here's a breakdown of how to manage cloud resources programmatically using Go:

1. Choose the Right Tools

Cloud SDKs: Each major cloud provider offers Go SDKs for interacting with their services.

AWS SDK for Go: `github.com/aws/aws-sdk-go`

Azure SDK for Go: `github.com/Azure/azure-sdk-for-go`

Google Cloud Client Libraries for Go: `cloud.google.com/go`

Infrastructure-as-Code (IaC) Tools: IaC tools like Terraform allow you to define and manage cloud infrastructure in a declarative manner. Many of these tools have Go providers or offer ways to interact with them programmatically.

2. Common Management Tasks

Provisioning:

Create and configure virtual machines, storage buckets, databases, networks, and other resources.

Define infrastructure using code (IaC) and automate its deployment.

Configuration:

Modify resource settings, such as instance types, security groups, and access policies.

Scaling:

Automatically adjust resources based on demand (e.g., scale up or down the number of instances in response to traffic).

Monitoring:

Collect metrics and logs from your cloud resources to track performance and identify issues.

Deleting:

Decommission resources that are no longer needed to optimize costs and avoid resource sprawl.

3. Example: Creating an AWS EC2 Instance

Go

```go
package main

import (

    "fmt"

    "github.com/aws/aws-sdk-go/aws"

    "github.com/aws/aws-sdk-go/aws/session"

    "github.com/aws/aws-sdk-go/service/ec2"

)
```

```go
func main() {

    sess, err := session.NewSession(&aws.Config{

        Region:   aws.String("us-west-2"),   //
Replace with your region

    })

    if err != nil {

        fmt.Println("Error  creating  session:",
err)

        return

    }


    svc := ec2.New(sess)


    result,                  err                 :=
svc.RunInstances(&ec2.RunInstancesInput{

        ImageId:
aws.String("ami-0c94855ba95c574c8"),   //  Replace
with your AMI ID

        InstanceType: aws.String("t2.micro"),

        MinCount:    aws.Int64(1),

        MaxCount:    aws.Int64(1),

    })

    if err != nil {
```

```
        fmt.Println("Error              launching
instance:", err)

        return

    }


    fmt.Println("Created              instance:",
*result.Instances[0].InstanceId)

}
```

This example uses the AWS SDK for Go to launch an EC2 instance with a specific AMI and instance type.

4. Best Practices

Idempotency: Design your code to be idempotent, so you can run it multiple times without unintended side effects.

Error Handling: Implement robust error handling to gracefully handle API failures or unexpected conditions.

State Management: Use appropriate techniques (e.g., databases, configuration files) to track the state of your cloud resources.

Security: Follow security best practices for managing cloud credentials and API access.

5. Benefits of Programmatic Management

Automation: Automate repetitive tasks, such as provisioning, configuration, and scaling.

Consistency: Ensure consistent configuration and deployment of cloud resources.

Scalability: Manage large numbers of resources efficiently.

Reduced Errors: Minimize manual errors and improve reliability.

Version Control: Track changes to your infrastructure using version control systems.

By using Go and the appropriate tools, you can effectively manage your cloud resources programmatically, enabling greater automation, efficiency, and control over your cloud environment.

5.3 Building Infrastructure-as-Code Tools with Go

Go is becoming increasingly popular for building Infrastructure-as-Code (IaC) tools, thanks to its efficiency, concurrency features, and strong ecosystem. Here's how you can leverage Go to create your own IaC tools:

1. Core Concepts

IaC: Managing and provisioning infrastructure through code instead of manual processes.

Declarative vs. Imperative:

Declarative: Define the desired state of your infrastructure (e.g., "I need 2 servers with these specs"), and the IaC tool figures out how to achieve it. (e.g., Terraform, Pulumi)

Imperative: Define the specific steps to create your infrastructure (e.g., "First create a network, then a server..."). (e.g., Ansible, Chef)

Benefits of IaC: Increased speed, consistency, reliability, reduced errors, version control, and improved collaboration.

2. Go's Advantages for IaC

Performance: Go's compiled nature and efficient memory management make it fast for processing infrastructure definitions and executing tasks.

Concurrency: Goroutines enable parallel execution of tasks, improving the speed of provisioning and managing resources.

Strong Standard Library: Go's standard library provides robust support for networking, file system interaction, and API communication, which are essential for IaC tools.

Ecosystem: Go has a growing ecosystem of libraries for interacting with cloud providers, configuration management tools, and other infrastructure components.

3. Building IaC Tools with Go

Define Infrastructure as Data: Use Go structs, maps, or other data structures to represent your infrastructure. You can use YAML, JSON, or other formats to define this data.

Create a Domain-Specific Language (DSL): If you need a more user-friendly way to define infrastructure, consider creating a DSL in Go using techniques like parser generators or custom parsing logic.

Implement Provisioning Logic: Write Go functions to interact with cloud provider APIs or configuration management tools to create, modify, and delete resources.

Add State Management: Implement state management to track the current state of your infrastructure and ensure idempotent operations.

Build a CLI: Create a command-line interface (CLI) for your IaC tool using libraries like `spf13/cobra` or `urfave/cli`.

4. Example: Simple IaC Tool for Creating AWS S3 Buckets

Go

```go
package main

import (

    "fmt"

    "github.com/aws/aws-sdk-go/aws"

    "github.com/aws/aws-sdk-go/aws/session"

    "github.com/aws/aws-sdk-go/service/s3"

)


type BucketConfig struct {

    Name    string `yaml:"name"`

    Region string `yaml:"region"`

}


func createBucket(sess *session.Session, config BucketConfig) error {

    svc := s3.New(sess)

    _, err := svc.CreateBucket(&s3.CreateBucketInput{
```

```go
            Bucket: aws.String(config.Name),

            CreateBucketConfiguration:
&s3.CreateBucketConfiguration{

                LocationConstraint:
aws.String(config.Region),

            },

        })

        return err

}


func main() {

        // ... load bucket configurations from YAML
...


        sess, _ := session.NewSession()


        for _, bucketConfig := range buckets {

            err := createBucket(sess, bucketConfig)

            if err != nil {

                fmt.Println("Error          creating
bucket:", err)

            } else {
```

```
                fmt.Println("Created      bucket:",
bucketConfig.Name)

        }

    }

}
```

This example defines a `BucketConfig` struct to represent S3 bucket configurations and a `createBucket()` function to create buckets using the AWS SDK.

5. Popular Go IaC Tools and Libraries

Terraform: Widely used IaC tool with Go providers for various cloud platforms and services.

Pulumi: Modern IaC platform that allows you to use Go (and other languages) to define infrastructure.

Crossplane: Framework for building cloud control planes with Kubernetes.

`hashicorp/terraform`: Go libraries for interacting with Terraform programmatically.

By combining Go's strengths with the right libraries and design principles, you can create powerful and efficient IaC tools to automate your infrastructure management and improve your DevOps workflows.

Chapter 6

Containerization with Go and Docker

6.1 Understanding Docker and Containerization

1. What is Containerization?

Traditional Virtual Machines: VMs emulate an entire operating system (OS), including the kernel, which leads to significant overhead.

Containers: Containers share the host OS kernel but provide isolated user spaces for applications. This makes them much lighter and faster than VMs.

Benefits:

Portability: "Build once, run anywhere" – containers run consistently across different environments (laptop, server, cloud).

Efficiency: Less overhead means you can run more containers on the same hardware compared to VMs.

Consistency: Provides a consistent environment for development, testing, and production.

Isolation: Applications are isolated from each other, preventing conflicts.

2. What is Docker?

Industry-Standard Containerization Platform: Docker is the most popular containerization platform. It provides tools for building, running, and managing containers.

Key Components:

Docker Engine: The core runtime environment for containers.

Docker Images: Read-only templates that define the container's file system, dependencies, and runtime environment.

Docker Containers: Running instances of Docker images.

Docker Hub: A registry for storing and sharing Docker images.

Dockerfile: A text file that contains instructions for building a Docker image.

3. How Docker Works

Dockerfile: You create a `Dockerfile` with instructions to build an image (e.g., specify the base image, copy files, install dependencies, set environment variables).

`docker build`: This command builds a Docker image from your `Dockerfile`.

`docker run`: This command creates and starts a container from an image.

Container Isolation: Docker uses Linux kernel features like namespaces and cgroups to isolate containers.

4. Key Docker Concepts

Layers: Docker images are built in layers, making them efficient to store and distribute. Each instruction in a `Dockerfile` creates a new layer.

Image Registry: A central location for storing and sharing Docker images (e.g., Docker Hub, Amazon ECR, Google Container Registry).

Volumes: Provide persistent storage for containers, allowing data to persist even if the container is deleted.

Networks: Allow containers to communicate with each other and the outside world.

5. Why Docker is Important for DevOps

Simplified Development: Provides a consistent development environment.

Microservices: Enables easy packaging and deployment of microservices.

Continuous Integration/Continuous Delivery (CI/CD): Integrates seamlessly with CI/CD pipelines for automated builds and deployments.

Cloud-Native Development: Docker is a foundation for cloud-native technologies like Kubernetes.

Example: Simple Dockerfile

Dockerfile

```
FROM ubuntu:latest

RUN apt-get update && apt-get install -y python3

COPY . /app

WORKDIR /app

CMD ["python3", "my_app.py"]
```

This `Dockerfile` starts with an Ubuntu base image, installs Python, copies the application code, and sets the command to run the Python script.

By understanding Docker and containerization, you'll be well-equipped to leverage these powerful technologies to streamline your development, deployment, and management of applications.

6.2 Automating Docker Builds and Deployments with Go

Go's ability to interact with the Docker Engine API and execute shell commands makes it a great choice for automating Docker builds and deployments. Here's how you can leverage Go for this purpose:

1. Use the Docker Engine API

`github.com/docker/docker/client`: This official Go library provides functions to interact with the Docker Engine API. You can use it to build images, manage containers, and perform other Docker operations programmatically.

Example: Building a Docker image

Go

```go
package main


import (

    "context"

    "fmt"
```

```go
    "io"

    "os"


    "github.com/docker/docker/api/types"

    "github.com/docker/docker/client"
)



func main() {

    ctx := context.Background()

    cli, err :=
client.NewClientWithOpts(client.FromEnv)

    if err != nil {

        panic(err)

    }



    tar, err := archive.TarWithOptions(".",
&archive.TarOptions{})

    if err != nil {

        panic(err)

    }
```

```go
	opts := types.ImageBuildOptions{

		Dockerfile: "Dockerfile",

		Tags:
[]string{"my-image:latest"},

	}


	res, err := cli.ImageBuild(ctx, tar, opts)

	if err != nil {

		panic(err)

	}

	defer res.Body.Close()


	io.Copy(os.Stdout, res.Body)

}
```

This example uses the Docker client to build an image from a Dockerfile in the current directory.

2. Execute Docker Commands

os/exec: You can use the exec.Command() function to execute Docker commands from your Go code, similar to how you would run them in a terminal.

Example: Building and pushing an image

Go

```go
package main

import (

    "fmt"

    "os/exec"

)


func main() {

    // Build the image

    buildCmd := exec.Command("docker", "build", "-t", "my-image:latest", ".")

    buildOut, err := buildCmd.CombinedOutput()

    if err != nil {

        fmt.Println("Error building image:", err)

        fmt.Println(string(buildOut))

        return

    }
```

```go
    // Push the image

    pushCmd := exec.Command("docker", "push",
"my-image:latest")

    pushOut, err := pushCmd.CombinedOutput()

    if err != nil {

        fmt.Println("Error pushing image:",
err)

        fmt.Println(string(pushOut))

        return

    }


    fmt.Println("Image built and pushed
successfully!")

}
```

This example builds an image and pushes it to a registry using `docker build` and `docker push` commands.

3. Automate Deployments

Combine with other tools: Use Go to integrate Docker with other DevOps tools like Kubernetes, Ansible, or Terraform for automated deployments.

Create deployment scripts: Write Go scripts to automate the entire deployment process, including building images, pushing them to a registry, and deploying them to your target environment.

4. Best Practices

Error Handling: Implement robust error handling to gracefully handle failures during builds or deployments.

Logging: Add logging to your Go code to track the progress of builds and deployments.

Security: Securely store Docker credentials and avoid hardcoding them in your code.

CI/CD Integration: Integrate your Go automation scripts with your CI/CD pipelines for automated builds and deployments on every code change.

By combining Go's capabilities with the Docker Engine API and other DevOps tools, you can create powerful automation solutions for building, deploying, and managing Docker containers, significantly improving your development and deployment workflows.

6.3 Managing Container Orchestration with Go

Go is a powerful language for managing container orchestration, thanks to its concurrency features, efficient networking capabilities, and excellent support for interacting with orchestration APIs. Here's how you can leverage Go to work with container orchestrators:

1. Understanding Container Orchestration

What it is: Automating the deployment, scaling, and management of containers.

Benefits:

Simplified management: Handles complex tasks like scheduling, scaling, networking, and health checks.

High availability: Ensures your applications are always running, even if containers or nodes fail.

Efficient resource utilization: Optimizes resource allocation across your cluster.

Scalability: Easily scale your applications up or down based on demand.

2. Popular Container Orchestrators

Kubernetes: The most popular container orchestrator. Provides a rich set of features for managing containerized applications.

Docker Swarm: A simpler orchestrator built into Docker Engine.

Nomad: A flexible and lightweight orchestrator by HashiCorp.

3. Using Go with Kubernetes

`k8s.io/client-go`: This official Go client library allows you to interact with the Kubernetes API. You can use it to:

Create, update, and delete pods, deployments, services, and other Kubernetes resources.

Monitor the state of your cluster and applications.

Automate deployments and rollouts.

Extend Kubernetes with custom controllers and operators.

Example: Listing Kubernetes Pods

```
Go

package main


import (
```

```go
    "context"

    "fmt"

    metav1
"k8s.io/apimachinery/pkg/apis/meta/v1"

    "k8s.io/client-go/kubernetes"

    "k8s.io/client-go/tools/clientcmd"

)


func main() {

    config,                  err                :=
clientcmd.BuildConfigFromFlags("",
"/path/to/your/kubeconfig")  // Update  with  your
kubeconfig path

    if err != nil {

        panic(err.Error())

    }


    clientset,               err                :=
kubernetes.NewForConfig(config)

    if err != nil {

        panic(err.Error())

    }
```

```
    pods,                  err              :=
clientset.CoreV1().Pods("").List(context.TODO(),
metav1.ListOptions{})

    if err != nil {

        panic(err.Error())

    }

    fmt.Printf("There   are   %d   pods   in   the
cluster\n", len(pods.Items))


    for _, pod := range pods.Items {

        fmt.Println(pod.Name)

    }

}
```

This example retrieves and lists all pods in your Kubernetes cluster.

4. Using Go with Other Orchestrators

Docker Swarm: Use the Docker Engine API (github.com/docker/docker/client) to manage Swarm services and tasks.

Nomad: Use the Nomad API client library (github.com/hashicorp/nomad/api) to interact with Nomad jobs and deployments.

5. Building Custom Orchestration Tools

Go's concurrency features: Leverage goroutines and channels to build efficient and scalable orchestration tools.

Custom logic: Implement custom logic for scheduling, scaling, and managing containers based on your specific needs.

Integrate with other systems: Integrate your orchestration tools with monitoring systems, logging platforms, and other DevOps tools.

6. Best Practices

Error Handling: Implement robust error handling to gracefully handle API failures and unexpected conditions.

Security: Securely manage API credentials and access to your orchestration platform.

Observability: Add logging and metrics to your orchestration tools to monitor their performance and health.

By using Go and its ecosystem of libraries, you can effectively manage container orchestration, automate deployments, and build custom tools to enhance your containerized workflows.

Chapter 7

Go for Configuration Management

7.1 Working with Configuration Management Tools (Ansible, Chef, Puppet)

Go can be a powerful tool when used in conjunction with configuration management tools like Ansible, Chef, and Puppet. While these tools have their own languages and ecosystems, Go can complement them in several ways:

1. Extending Functionality

Custom Modules/Plugins: You can write custom modules or plugins in Go to extend the functionality of these tools. This is particularly useful when you need to perform tasks that are not readily available in the built-in modules or when you need to integrate with systems that have Go APIs.

Ansible: Write Go plugins for actions, filters, or modules.

Chef: Create custom resources and providers in Go.

Puppet: Develop custom functions and types in Go.

2. Automating Workflows

Wrapper Scripts: Write Go scripts to automate interactions with these configuration management tools. This can include:

Running playbooks (Ansible) or recipes (Chef) with specific parameters.

Orchestrating complex workflows involving multiple tools or stages.

Generating configuration files or templates dynamically.

3. Integrating with APIs

API Clients: Use Go to build API clients for interacting with the APIs provided by these tools. This allows you to:

Programmatically manage nodes, environments, and configurations.

Retrieve information about the state of your infrastructure.

Trigger actions or workflows remotely.

4. Building Custom Tools

Go as the Orchestrator: Use Go as the central orchestrator for your configuration management tasks, even if the core configuration logic is handled by Ansible, Chef, or Puppet. Go can handle tasks like:

Inventory management.

Deployment orchestration.

Reporting and monitoring.

5. Example: Running an Ansible Playbook with Go

Go

```go
package main


import (

    "fmt"

    "os/exec"

)
```

```go
func main() {

    cmd    :=    exec.Command("ansible-playbook",
"my_playbook.yml", "-i", "inventory.ini")

    out, err := cmd.CombinedOutput()

    if err != nil {

        fmt.Println("Error  running  playbook:",
err)

        fmt.Println(string(out))

        return

    }



    fmt.Println("Playbook ran successfully:")

    fmt.Println(string(out))

}
```

This example uses the `exec.Command()` function to run an Ansible playbook with a specified inventory file.

6. Benefits of Using Go

Performance: Go's speed and efficiency can improve the performance of your configuration management workflows.

Concurrency: Goroutines enable parallel execution of tasks, which can speed up configuration management operations, especially when dealing with a large number of nodes.

Cross-Platform Compatibility: Go's ability to compile to different platforms allows you to build tools that work across various operating systems.

Important Considerations:

Tool-Specific Knowledge: You'll need to understand the core concepts and languages of Ansible, Chef, or Puppet to effectively extend or integrate with them.

API Availability: Ensure that the configuration management tool you're using has a well-documented API or provides ways to extend its functionality.

By combining Go with configuration management tools, you can create more powerful, flexible, and efficient solutions for managing and automating your infrastructure.

7.2 Writing Custom Configuration Management Modules in Go

Go's versatility allows you to create custom configuration management modules that integrate seamlessly with popular tools like Ansible, Chef, and Puppet. These modules can extend the functionality of these tools, enabling you to automate tasks specific to your infrastructure or applications.

Here's a breakdown of how to write custom configuration management modules in Go:

1. Understand the Tool's Module Structure

Ansible: Ansible modules typically accept input as JSON arguments and return output in JSON format. They are often written as standalone executable scripts.

Chef: Chef custom resources are defined using Ruby DSL, but the underlying providers that perform the actual work can be written in Go.

Puppet: Puppet custom functions and types can be written in Go and integrated into Puppet manifests.

2. Implement the Module Logic in Go

Input Processing: Parse input arguments or data structures provided by the configuration management tool.

Core Logic: Implement the core logic of your module in Go. This might involve interacting with APIs, managing files, running commands, or performing other system-level tasks.

Output Formatting: Format the output of your module according to the requirements of the configuration management tool (e.g., JSON for Ansible).

3. Example: Ansible Module for Checking Service Status

Go

```
package main

import (

    "encoding/json"

    "fmt"

    "os"
```

```go
    "os/exec"

)


type ModuleInput struct {

    Name string `json:"name"`

}


type ModuleOutput struct {

    Status  string `json:"status"`

    Changed bool    `json:"changed"`

}


func main() {

    var input ModuleInput

    json.Unmarshal([]byte(os.Getenv("INPUT")),
&input)


    cmd        :=         exec.Command("systemctl",
"is-active", input.Name)

    out, err := cmd.CombinedOutput()
```

```go
    output := ModuleOutput{Changed: false}

    if err != nil {

        output.Status = "inactive"

    } else {

        output.Status = "active"

    }


    jsonOutput, _ := json.Marshal(output)

    fmt.Println(string(jsonOutput))

}
```

This example demonstrates a simple Ansible module that checks the status of a systemd service. It receives the service name as input, uses `systemctl` to check its status, and returns the status in JSON format.

4. Testing and Packaging

Unit Tests: Write unit tests in Go to ensure the correctness of your module's logic.

Integration Tests: Test your module with the configuration management tool to verify its integration and functionality.

Packaging: Package your Go module in a way that is compatible with the configuration management tool (e.g., as a standalone executable for Ansible).

5. Benefits of Using Go

Performance: Go's compiled nature and efficient execution can improve the performance of your custom modules.

Cross-Platform Compatibility: Write modules that can run on different operating systems.

Access to Go Ecosystem: Leverage Go's extensive ecosystem of libraries for tasks like API interaction, networking, and system management.

Important Considerations:

Tool-Specific Requirements: Adhere to the specific requirements and guidelines for writing modules for your chosen configuration management tool.

Error Handling: Implement robust error handling to provide informative feedback to the configuration management tool.

By writing custom configuration management modules in Go, you can extend the capabilities of your existing tools and automate a wider range of tasks, tailoring them to your specific infrastructure needs.

7.3 Automating Configuration Management Workflows

Go's strengths in concurrency, automation, and API interaction make it well-suited for orchestrating and automating configuration management workflows. Here's how you can leverage Go to streamline your configuration management processes:

1. Define Workflows

Represent Workflows as Code: Use Go to define your configuration management workflows as code. You can use simple scripts, functions, or even create custom DSLs (Domain-Specific Languages) for more complex workflows.

Structure with Goroutines: Leverage goroutines and channels to execute tasks concurrently, improving the speed and efficiency of your workflows.

Break Down into Stages: Divide your workflows into logical stages (e.g., provisioning, configuration, deployment, testing) for better organization and maintainability.

2. Interact with Configuration Management Tools

Execute Commands: Use the `os/exec` package to execute commands for tools like Ansible, Chef, or Puppet.

API Integration: Use Go to interact with the APIs provided by these tools, enabling programmatic control over nodes, environments, and configurations.

Custom Modules: Write custom modules in Go to extend the functionality of your configuration management tools.

3. Manage State and Dependencies

Track State: Use Go to track the state of your infrastructure and configuration changes. This can involve storing state information in files, databases, or using tools like etcd or Consul.

Handle Dependencies: Ensure that tasks are executed in the correct order based on their dependencies. Go's concurrency features can help with managing parallel execution while respecting dependencies.

4. Incorporate Error Handling and Logging

Robust Error Handling: Implement comprehensive error handling to gracefully handle failures and prevent your workflows from crashing.

Detailed Logging: Add logging to your Go code to track the progress of your workflows and provide insights into any issues that may arise.

5. Example: Automating a Deployment Workflow

Go

```go
package main

import (

    "fmt"

    "os/exec"

)


func provisionServers() error {

    // ... use Go to provision servers (e.g.,
with Terraform or cloud provider APIs) ...

    return nil

}


func runAnsiblePlaybook() error {

    cmd    :=    exec.Command("ansible-playbook",
"deploy.yml")

    out, err := cmd.CombinedOutput()
```

```go
        if err != nil {

                fmt.Println("Error  running  Ansible:",
err)

                fmt.Println(string(out))

                return err

        }

        return nil

}


func runTests() error {

        // ... use Go to run tests ...

        return nil

}


func main() {

        err := provisionServers()

        if err != nil {

                return

        }


        err = runAnsiblePlaybook()
```

```
if err != nil {

    return

}


err = runTests()

if err != nil {

    return

}



fmt.Println("Deployment   workflow   completed
successfully!")

}
```

This simplified example demonstrates a deployment workflow that provisions servers, runs an Ansible playbook for configuration, and then executes tests.

6. Benefits of Automation

Increased Speed and Efficiency: Automate repetitive tasks and speed up your workflows.

Reduced Errors: Minimize manual errors and ensure consistent configurations.

Improved Collaboration: Define workflows as code for better collaboration and version control.

Scalability: Handle complex configuration management tasks for large-scale infrastructure.

By using Go to automate your configuration management workflows, you can improve the efficiency, reliability, and scalability of your infrastructure management processes, allowing you to focus on more strategic initiatives.

Chapter 8

CI/CD Pipelines with Go

8.1 Building Continuous Integration Pipelines

Go's ability to automate tasks, interact with APIs, and manage processes makes it a valuable asset for building continuous integration (CI) pipelines. Here's how you can leverage Go to create robust and efficient CI pipelines:

1. Core CI Concepts

Continuous Integration: A development practice where developers integrate code changes into a shared repository frequently, triggering automated builds and tests to detect errors early.

Key Steps in a CI Pipeline:

Code Fetch: Retrieve the latest code changes from a version control system (e.g., Git).

Build: Compile the code and create any necessary artifacts (e.g., executables, libraries, Docker images).

Test: Run automated tests (unit tests, integration tests) to verify the code's correctness.

Report: Generate reports on the build and test results.

(Optional) Deploy: Deploy the built artifacts to a staging environment for further testing.

2. Go's Strengths for CI

Automation: Go excels at automating tasks, making it ideal for orchestrating the steps in a CI pipeline.

API Interaction: Go can interact with APIs of version control systems (e.g., GitHub, GitLab), build tools, testing frameworks, and deployment platforms.

Concurrency: Goroutines enable parallel execution of tasks, such as running tests concurrently to speed up the pipeline.

Cross-Platform Compatibility: Build CI pipelines that work across different operating systems.

3. Building CI Pipelines with Go

Orchestrate with Go: Use Go to write scripts or programs that orchestrate the different stages of your CI pipeline.

Execute Commands: Use the `os/exec` package to execute commands for build tools, testing frameworks, linters, and other tools in your pipeline.

Interact with APIs: Use Go to interact with APIs to trigger builds, fetch test results, and update the status of your CI pipeline in your version control system.

Integrate with CI Tools: Go can be used to extend or integrate with existing CI tools like Jenkins, GitLab CI, or CircleCI.

4. Example: Simple CI Pipeline in Go

Go

```
package main

import (

    "fmt"

    "os/exec"

)
```

```go
func fetchCode() error {

    // ... use `os/exec` or a Git library to
    fetch the latest code ...

    return nil

}


func buildProject() error {

    cmd := exec.Command("go", "build")

    // ... handle output and errors ...

    return nil

}


func runTests() error {

    cmd := exec.Command("go", "test", "./...")

    // ... handle output and errors ...

    return nil

}


func main() {

    err := fetchCode()
```

```
    if err != nil {

        // ... handle error ...

    }


    err = buildProject()

    if err != nil {

        // ... handle error ...

    }


    err = runTests()

    if err != nil {

        // ... handle error ...

    }


    // ... report results ...

}
```

This example outlines a basic CI pipeline that fetches code, builds the project, and runs tests.

5. Best Practices

Keep it Simple: Start with a simple pipeline and gradually add complexity as needed.

Modularize: Break down your pipeline into modular functions or scripts for better organization and reusability.

Error Handling: Implement robust error handling to gracefully handle failures and provide informative feedback.

Logging: Add logging to your Go code to track the progress of your CI pipeline and troubleshoot issues.

By using Go to build your CI pipelines, you gain greater control, flexibility, and efficiency in your continuous integration process. You can tailor your pipelines to your specific needs and integrate them seamlessly with your existing development workflows.

8.2 Automating Deployment Processes

Go's strengths in automation, concurrency, and API interaction make it a powerful tool for automating deployment processes. Here's a breakdown of how you can leverage Go to streamline your deployments:

1. Define Deployment Steps

Represent Deployments as Code: Use Go to define your deployment steps as code. This can involve creating functions or scripts that automate tasks like building artifacts, transferring files, configuring servers, and restarting services.

Structure with Goroutines: Leverage goroutines and channels to execute deployment tasks concurrently, improving speed and efficiency.

Modularize for Reusability: Break down your deployment process into modular functions or scripts that can be reused across different projects or environments.

2. Interact with Deployment Targets

SSH: Use the `golang.org/x/crypto/ssh` package to execute commands and transfer files over SSH to your servers.

Cloud Provider APIs: Use cloud provider SDKs (AWS SDK for Go, Azure SDK for Go, etc.) to interact with cloud services and automate deployments to cloud environments.

Container Orchestration: Use Kubernetes client libraries (`k8s.io/client-go`) or Docker Engine API (`github.com/docker/docker/client`) to automate deployments to containerized environments.

3. Manage Deployments

Rollouts and Rollbacks: Implement strategies for rolling out deployments gradually (e.g., canary deployments, blue/green deployments) and rolling back to previous versions if issues occur.

Configuration Management: Integrate with configuration management tools like Ansible, Chef, or Puppet to automate server configuration and application setup.

Monitoring and Logging: Add monitoring and logging to your deployment process to track progress, identify issues, and ensure successful deployments.

4. Example: Simple Deployment Script

```go
Go

package main


import (
```

```go
    "fmt"

    "os/exec"

)


func buildArtifact() error {

    cmd := exec.Command("go", "build")

    // ... handle output and errors ...

    return nil

}


func transferArtifact(host string) error {

    // ... use `scp` or
`golang.org/x/crypto/ssh` to transfer the
artifact ...

    return nil

}


func restartService(host string) error {

    // ... use SSH to restart the service on the
remote host ...

    return nil

}
```

```go
func main() {

    err := buildArtifact()

    if err != nil {

        // ... handle error ...

    }


    err = transferArtifact("your-server-ip")

    if err != nil {

        // ... handle error ...

    }


    err = restartService("your-server-ip")

    if err != nil {

        // ... handle error ...

    }


    fmt.Println("Deployment                completed
successfully!")

}
```

This example outlines a basic deployment script that builds an artifact, transfers it to a server, and restarts a service.

5. Best Practices

Idempotency: Design your deployment scripts to be idempotent so they can be run multiple times without unintended side effects.

Error Handling: Implement robust error handling to gracefully handle failures during deployments.

Security: Securely manage credentials and avoid hardcoding sensitive information in your deployment scripts.

CI/CD Integration: Integrate your deployment scripts with your CI/CD pipelines for automated deployments on every code change.

By automating your deployment processes with Go, you can improve the speed, reliability, and consistency of your deployments, reducing manual errors and freeing up your team to focus on other tasks.

8.3 Integrating Go with CI/CD Tools (Jenkins, GitLab CI, CircleCI)

Go's flexibility and ability to interact with various systems make it a great choice for integrating with popular CI/CD tools like Jenkins, GitLab CI, and CircleCI. Here's how you can leverage Go in your CI/CD workflows:

1. Jenkins

Go Plugins for Jenkins: You can write Jenkins plugins in Go to extend Jenkins functionality. These plugins can:

Execute custom build steps.

Integrate with other tools or services.

Provide custom visualizations or reports.

Jenkins API Client: Use the Jenkins API client library (github.com/bndr/gojenkins) to interact with Jenkins programmatically. This allows you to:

Trigger builds.

Retrieve build information and artifacts.

Manage jobs and pipelines.

Example: Triggering a Jenkins build with Go

Go

```go
package main


import (

    "fmt"

    "github.com/bndr/gojenkins"

)



func main() {

    jenkins := gojenkins.CreateJenkins(nil,
"http://your-jenkins-server", "username",
"password")

    // ... error handling ...


    _, err := jenkins.BuildJob("your-job-name")
```

```
    if err != nil {

        // ... handle error ...

    }


    fmt.Println("Jenkins     build     triggered
successfully!")

}
```

2. GitLab CI

Go Runners: GitLab CI uses runners to execute jobs. You can create custom runners in Go to execute specific build or deployment tasks.

GitLab API Client: Use the GitLab API client library (github.com/xanzy/go-gitlab) to interact with GitLab programmatically. This allows you to:

Trigger pipelines.

Retrieve pipeline status and logs.

Manage projects and repositories.

3. CircleCI

CircleCI API Client: Use the CircleCI API client library (github.com/CircleCI-Public/circleci-cli) to interact with CircleCI programmatically. This allows you to:

Trigger workflows.

Retrieve workflow status and artifacts.

Manage projects and contexts.

Orbs: CircleCI Orbs are reusable packages of configuration. You can create custom Orbs in Go to share common build or deployment steps across projects.

General Integration Strategies

Execute Commands: Use the `os/exec` package to execute commands for tools like `go build`, `go test`, or other CLI tools within your CI/CD pipelines.

Generate Configuration Files: Use Go to generate configuration files dynamically for your CI/CD tools.

Create Custom Tools: Build custom tools in Go to enhance your CI/CD workflows. This could include tools for:

Analyzing code quality.

Managing deployments.

Generating reports.

Benefits of Using Go

Flexibility: Go's versatility allows you to integrate with various CI/CD tools and customize your workflows.

Performance: Go's efficiency can improve the performance of your CI/CD pipelines.

Maintainability: Represent your CI/CD logic as Go code for better maintainability and version control.

By integrating Go with your CI/CD tools, you can create more efficient, flexible, and powerful automation workflows, streamlining your development and deployment processes.

Chapter 9

Monitoring and Observability with Go

9.1 Implementing Monitoring and Logging in Go Applications

Effective monitoring and logging are crucial for maintaining the health and performance of your Go applications. Here's how to implement them effectively:

1. Logging

Standard Library (`log`)

Provides basic logging functionality with functions like `Println()`, `Printf()`, `Fatalf()`.

You can configure output to different writers (files, network) and set prefixes.

Example:

Go

```go
import "log"


log.Println("This is an informational message.")

log.Printf("The value of x is %d", x)
```

Third-Party Logging Libraries

Logrus (`github.com/sirupsen/logrus`): Popular, feature-rich library with structured logging, log levels, hooks (for sending logs to external systems), and formatters.

Zap (`go.uber.org/zap`): High-performance logging library focused on speed and structured logging.

Zerolog (`github.com/rs/zerolog`): Fast and lightweight JSON logger.

Best Practices

Structured Logging: Use structured logging (JSON format) for easier parsing and analysis.

Log Levels: Use different log levels (DEBUG, INFO, WARN, ERROR) to categorize log messages by severity.

Contextual Information: Include relevant context (request IDs, timestamps, user IDs) in your logs.

Log Management: Use a centralized log management system (e.g., ELK stack, Splunk) to collect, store, and analyze logs.

2. Monitoring

Metrics

Counters: Count events (e.g., number of requests, errors).

Gauges: Measure values at a specific point in time (e.g., CPU usage, memory usage).

Histograms: Track the distribution of values (e.g., request latency).

Metrics Libraries

Prometheus (`github.com/prometheus/client_golang`): Popular open-source monitoring system with a Go client library.

Expvar: Standard library package for exporting metrics in a format that can be consumed by monitoring tools.

Monitoring Tools

Prometheus: Collects, stores, and queries metrics.

Grafana: Creates dashboards and visualizations from metrics.

3. Tracing

Distributed Tracing: Track requests as they flow through your application, especially in microservices architectures.

OpenTracing and Jaeger: OpenTracing is a standard for distributed tracing. Jaeger is a popular open-source tracing system.

4. Health Checks

`/healthz` **Endpoint:** Create an HTTP endpoint (`/healthz`) that returns the health status of your application.

Check Dependencies: Include checks for database connections, external services, and other critical components.

Example: Using Prometheus for Monitoring

Go

```
package main
```

```go
import (

    "net/http"


"github.com/prometheus/client_golang/prometheus"


"github.com/prometheus/client_golang/prometheus/p
romhttp"

)



var (

    requestsCounter = prometheus.NewCounterVec(

        prometheus.CounterOpts{

            Name: "my_app_requests_total",

            Help: "Total  number  of  requests
processed by the application.",

        },

        []string{"endpoint"},

    )

)



func main() {
```

```go
    prometheus.MustRegister(requestsCounter)


    http.HandleFunc("/",                            func(w
http.ResponseWriter, r *http.Request) {


requestsCounter.WithLabelValues("/").Inc()

        // ... your handler logic ...

    })



    http.Handle("/metrics", promhttp.Handler())

    http.ListenAndServe(":8080", nil)

}
```

This example uses the Prometheus Go client library to create a counter for tracking HTTP requests and exposes the metrics at `/metrics`.

5. Key Considerations

Contextual Logging: Use request IDs or correlation IDs to track requests across different services.

Performance: Be mindful of the performance impact of logging and monitoring. Use efficient logging libraries and avoid excessive logging.

Security: Protect sensitive information in logs and metrics.

Alerting: Configure alerts based on metrics or log events to notify you of potential issues.

By implementing comprehensive monitoring and logging in your Go applications, you gain valuable insights into their behavior, identify issues proactively, and ensure their reliability and performance.

9.2 Integrating with Monitoring Systems (Prometheus, Grafana)

Integrating your Go applications with monitoring systems like Prometheus and Grafana is essential for gaining insights into their performance, health, and behavior. Here's how to do it effectively:

1. Prometheus Integration

`github.com/prometheus/client_golang`: This is the official Go client library for Prometheus. It provides tools for instrumenting your Go code and exposing metrics in a format that Prometheus can scrape.

Key components:

Metrics: Define various metric types (counters, gauges, histograms, summaries) using the `prometheus` package.

Collectors: Register collectors to gather and expose metrics from your application.

HTTP Handler: Expose a `/metrics` endpoint using `promhttp.Handler()` to allow Prometheus to scrape your metrics.

Example:

Go

```
package main
```

```go
import (

    "net/http"


    "github.com/prometheus/client_golang/prometheus"

    "github.com/prometheus/client_golang/prometheus/p
romhttp"
)


var (

    httpRequestsTotal = prometheus.NewCounterVec(

        prometheus.CounterOpts{

            Name: "http_requests_total",

            Help: "Total number of HTTP requests
processed.",

        },

        []string{"method", "path"},

    )

)
```

```go
func main() {

    prometheus.MustRegister(httpRequestsTotal)



                  http.HandleFunc("/",        func(w
http.ResponseWriter, r *http.Request) {


httpRequestsTotal.WithLabelValues(r.Method,
r.URL.Path).Inc()

        // ... your handler logic ...

    })



    http.Handle("/metrics", promhttp.Handler())

    http.ListenAndServe(":8080", nil)

}
```

This example creates a counter to track HTTP requests and exposes it at /metrics.

2. Grafana Integration

Data Source: Configure a Prometheus data source in Grafana to connect to your Prometheus server.

Dashboards and Panels: Create dashboards and panels in Grafana to visualize the metrics collected by Prometheus.

Use Grafana's query editor to select metrics and apply functions or transformations.

Choose from a variety of visualization types (graphs, gauges, heatmaps, etc.).

Alerting: Set up alerts in Grafana based on your Prometheus metrics to notify you of potential issues.

3. Best Practices

Meaningful Metric Names: Use clear and descriptive names for your metrics.

Labels: Use labels to add dimensions to your metrics (e.g., HTTP method, response code).

Histograms and Summaries: Use histograms and summaries to track the distribution of values like request latency.

Alerting Thresholds: Set appropriate thresholds for your alerts to avoid false positives.

4. Key Benefits

Visibility: Gain insights into your application's performance and behavior.

Troubleshooting: Use metrics and dashboards to diagnose and troubleshoot issues.

Proactive Monitoring: Set up alerts to be notified of potential problems before they impact users.

Performance Optimization: Identify bottlenecks and optimize your application's performance.

By integrating your Go applications with Prometheus and Grafana, you can establish a robust monitoring system that provides valuable insights and helps you maintain the health and performance of your applications.

9.3 Building Custom Monitoring and Alerting Tools

Go's flexibility and powerful libraries make it an excellent choice for building custom monitoring and alerting tools tailored to your specific needs. Here's a guide to get you started:

1. Define Monitoring Requirements

What to Monitor: Identify the key metrics and events you need to track (e.g., system metrics, application performance, custom events).

Alerting Conditions: Define the conditions that should trigger alerts (e.g., threshold breaches, unusual patterns, error rates).

Notification Channels: Determine how you want to receive alerts (e.g., email, Slack, PagerDuty).

2. Collect Data

System Metrics: Use Go packages like `os` and `gopsutil` to gather system-level metrics (CPU usage, memory, disk space).

Application Metrics: Instrument your Go applications to expose custom metrics using libraries like `expvar` or `prometheus/client_golang`.

Log Files: Parse and analyze log files to extract relevant information.

External APIs: Collect data from external APIs or services.

3. Process and Analyze Data

Store Data: Store collected data in a time-series database (e.g., InfluxDB, Prometheus) or a general-purpose database.

Analyze Data: Implement logic in Go to analyze data, identify trends, and detect anomalies.

Trigger Alerts: When alerting conditions are met, trigger notifications through your chosen channels.

4. Build Alerting Mechanisms

Email: Use `net/smtp` to send email alerts.

Slack: Integrate with the Slack API using a library like `slack-go/slack`.

PagerDuty: Use the PagerDuty API to trigger incidents.

Webhooks: Send HTTP POST requests to webhooks to trigger actions in other systems.

5. Create a User Interface (Optional)

Build a Web UI: Use Go web frameworks like Gin, Echo, or Chi to create a web UI for visualizing data and managing alerts.

CLI: Create a command-line interface (CLI) for interacting with your monitoring tool.

Example: Simple CPU Usage Monitor with Alerts

Go

```go
package main


import (

    "fmt"

    "time"


    "github.com/shirou/gopsutil/cpu"

    "github.com/go-mail/mail"
```

```go
)


func sendEmailAlert(subject, body string) error {

    m := mail.NewMessage()

    // ... configure email sender, recipient,
    subject, body ...

    return mail.Send(m)

}


func main() {

    for {

        percentages, err :=
    cpu.Percent(time.Second, true)

        if err != nil {

            // ... handle error ...

        }


        for i, cpuPercent := range percentages
    {

            if cpuPercent > 80 {

                err := sendEmailAlert("High
    CPU Usage Alert", fmt.Sprintf("CPU %d usage is
    %.2f%%", i, cpuPercent))
```

```go
        if err != nil {

            // ... handle error ...

        }

    }

}


    time.Sleep(5 * time.Second)

    }

}
```

This example monitors CPU usage and sends email alerts if any core exceeds 80% usage.

Key Considerations

Scalability: Design your tool to handle increasing amounts of data and alerts as your infrastructure grows.

Reliability: Ensure your monitoring tool is reliable and can handle failures gracefully.

Maintainability: Write clean, well-documented code for easier maintenance.

Security: Protect sensitive information (credentials, API keys) used by your tool.

By building custom monitoring and alerting tools with Go, you can tailor them precisely to your needs, integrate with your existing systems, and gain deeper insights into the health and performance of your infrastructure and applications.

Chapter 10

Advanced Go Techniques for DevOps

10.1 Concurrency and Goroutines for Efficient Automation

Go's built-in concurrency features, particularly goroutines and channels, are incredibly powerful for building efficient automation solutions. Here's how they contribute to efficient automation:

1. Goroutines: Lightweight Concurrency

Lightweight Threads: Goroutines are lightweight, concurrent execution units. They are similar to threads but much more lightweight, allowing you to create thousands or even millions of them without significant overhead.

Concurrent Execution: Goroutines allow you to execute multiple tasks seemingly at the same time. This is essential for automation tasks that involve:

Parallel Processing: Performing independent operations concurrently (e.g., processing multiple files, making API calls to different services).

Asynchronous Operations: Handling tasks that might take time to complete without blocking the main program (e.g., network requests, file I/O).

Simplified Concurrency: Go's syntax for creating goroutines is very simple:

Go

```
go func() {

    // Code to be executed in a goroutine

}()
```

2. Channels: Safe Communication

Communication Mechanism: Channels provide a safe and synchronized way for goroutines to communicate with each other.

Data Synchronization: Channels prevent race conditions and data corruption by ensuring that only one goroutine can access the data at a time.

Coordination: Channels can be used to coordinate the execution of goroutines, ensuring that tasks are completed in the correct order or that certain conditions are met before proceeding.

3. Efficient Automation with Goroutines and Channels

Parallel Tasks: Execute independent automation tasks in parallel using goroutines. For example, if you need to process a large number of files, you can create a goroutine for each file.

Asynchronous Operations: Handle long-running tasks asynchronously without blocking the main automation workflow. For example, you can use a goroutine to make an API call and use a channel to receive the result when it's available.

Real-time Monitoring: Create goroutines to continuously monitor systems or services and send alerts through channels when specific conditions are met.

Rate Limiting: Use channels to control the rate of API calls or other operations to avoid exceeding rate limits.

Example: Parallel File Processing

Go

```go
package main


import (

    "fmt"

    "sync"

)



func processFile(filename string, wg *sync.WaitGroup) {

    defer wg.Done()

    // ... process the file ...

    fmt.Println("Processed:", filename)

}



func main() {
```

```go
    files := []string{"file1.txt", "file2.txt",
"file3.txt"}

    var wg sync.WaitGroup

    wg.Add(len(files))


    for _, file := range files {

        go processFile(file, &wg)

    }


    wg.Wait()

    fmt.Println("All files processed.")

}
```

This example uses goroutines to process multiple files concurrently. The `sync.WaitGroup` is used to wait for all goroutines to finish before exiting the program.

Key Considerations

Error Handling: Implement proper error handling in goroutines to prevent panics and ensure that errors are propagated correctly.

Context: Use contexts to manage the lifecycle of goroutines and cancel them if necessary.

Synchronization: Use channels or other synchronization primitives (mutexes, semaphores) to coordinate access to shared resources and prevent race conditions.

By effectively utilizing goroutines and channels, you can create highly efficient and concurrent automation solutions in Go, improving the speed and responsiveness of your automation workflows.

10.2 Working with Go Templates for Code Generation

Go's template engine, found in the `text/template` package, is a powerful tool for code generation. It allows you to define templates with placeholders and logic, which can then be populated with data to generate various kinds of code. This can be extremely useful in DevOps for automating repetitive tasks, creating configuration files, and generating boilerplate code.

Here's a breakdown of how to use Go templates for code generation:

1. Create a Template

Define the Template: Create a template string with placeholders (using `{{ }}`) for dynamic content and control structures (e.g., `{{if}}`, `{{range}}`) for conditional logic and loops.

Parse the Template: Use `template.New("templateName").Parse(templateString)` to parse the template string and create a `template.Template` object.

2. Provide Data

Data Structures: Create Go structs, maps, or slices to hold the data that will be used to populate the template.

Example:

Go

```go
type ServerConfig struct {

    Name      string

    IP        string

    Port      int

}
```

3. Execute the Template

Populate Placeholders: Use `template.Execute(writer, data)` to execute the template, replacing placeholders with data from your data structures.

Output: The generated code will be written to the specified writer (e.g., a file, standard output).

Example: Generating Nginx Configuration Files

Go

```go
package main


import (

    "os"

    "text/template"

)
```

```go
type ServerConfig struct {

    ServerName string

    ServerIP   string

    Port       int

}


const nginxConfTemplate = `

server {

    listen       {{.Port}};

    server_name  {{.ServerName}};


    location / {

                            proxy_pass
http://{{.ServerIP}}:{{.Port}};

    }

}

`


func main() {

    servers := []ServerConfig{
```

```go
        {ServerName: "example.com", ServerIP:
"192.168.1.100", Port: 80},

        {ServerName:          "api.example.com",
ServerIP: "192.168.1.101", Port: 8080},

    }


    tmpl,                err                :=
template.New("nginx").Parse(nginxConfTemplate)

    if err != nil {

        panic(err)

    }


    for _, server := range servers {

        filename := server.ServerName + ".conf"

        file, err := os.Create(filename)

        if err != nil {

            panic(err)

        }

        defer file.Close()


        err = tmpl.Execute(file, server)

        if err != nil {
```

```go
        panic(err)

    }


    fmt.Println("Generated:", filename)

  }

}
```

This example generates Nginx configuration files for multiple servers based on the data in the `servers` slice.

Benefits of Using Go Templates for Code Generation

Automation: Automate the creation of repetitive code or configuration files.

Consistency: Ensure consistency in generated code.

Reduced Errors: Minimize manual errors and typos.

Maintainability: Manage templates separately from your main code for better organization.

Flexibility: Use conditional logic and loops to generate code dynamically.

Key Considerations

Template Design: Design your templates carefully to ensure they are easy to understand and maintain.

Error Handling: Implement error handling to gracefully handle template parsing or execution errors.

Security: Be mindful of potential security risks when generating code from external data.

By leveraging Go templates for code generation, you can significantly improve your productivity, reduce errors, and streamline your DevOps workflows.

10.3 Best Practices for Go DevOps Projects

When applying Go to DevOps projects, following best practices can significantly improve the quality, maintainability, and efficiency of your code and automation workflows. Here are some key recommendations:

1. Project Structure and Code Organization

Clear Directory Structure: Organize your project with a clear and consistent directory structure. Common directories include `cmd` (for main applications), `pkg` (for reusable packages), and `internal` (for internal packages).

Meaningful Package Names: Use concise and descriptive package names that reflect their purpose.

Code Formatting: Use `gofmt` to automatically format your code according to Go conventions.

Linting: Use linters like `golint` and `staticcheck` to identify potential code issues and enforce best practices.

2. Error Handling

Handle Errors Explicitly: Don't ignore errors. Handle them gracefully using `if err != nil { ... }`.

Provide Context: Add context to error messages to make them more informative.

Wrap Errors: Use `fmt.Errorf` or custom error types to wrap errors with additional context.

3. Concurrency

Avoid Race Conditions: Use channels, mutexes, or other synchronization primitives to prevent race conditions when accessing shared resources from multiple goroutines.

Context: Use contexts to manage the lifecycle of goroutines and cancel them when necessary.

Keep it Simple: Avoid overusing concurrency. Start with simple solutions and introduce concurrency only when needed for performance or responsiveness.

4. Testing

Write Unit Tests: Write comprehensive unit tests to ensure the correctness of your code.

Use Mocking: Use mocking libraries to isolate units of code during testing.

Integration Tests: Write integration tests to test the interactions between different components of your system.

5. Security

Secure Credentials: Don't hardcode sensitive information (API keys, passwords) in your code. Use environment variables, configuration files, or secrets management tools.

Least Privilege: Grant your Go applications only the necessary permissions they need to perform their tasks.

Input Validation: Validate all external input to prevent security vulnerabilities.

6. Documentation

Write Clear Comments: Document your code with clear and concise comments.

Generate Documentation: Use tools like `godoc` to generate documentation from your code comments.

README: Provide a comprehensive README file with instructions on how to build, run, and use your project.

7. Deployment and Monitoring

Containerization: Containerize your Go applications using Docker for easier deployment and portability.

Orchestration: Use container orchestration tools like Kubernetes to manage and scale your deployments.

Monitoring and Logging: Integrate monitoring and logging into your Go applications to track their performance and health.

8. Tools and Libraries

Dependency Management: Use a dependency management tool like `go mod` to manage your project's dependencies.

Build Tools: Use build tools like `make` or `go build` to automate the build process.

CI/CD: Integrate your Go projects with CI/CD pipelines for automated builds, tests, and deployments.

By following these best practices, you can create Go DevOps projects that are well-structured, maintainable, efficient, and secure. This will help you build robust automation solutions and improve your overall DevOps workflows.